D1230504

j/535.6/D

DISCARDED OR WITHDR
GREAT NECK LIBRAR

APR 1 5 2015

GREAT NECK LIBRARY
GREAT NECK, NY 11023
(516) 466-8055
Renew your books online at:
www.greatnecklibrary.org

Black
Seeing Black All around Us

by Michael Dahl

Consulting Editor: Gail Saunders-Smith, PhD

Great Neck Library

Capstone press

Mankato, Minnesota

A+ Books are published by Capstone Press,
151 Good Counsel Drive, P.O. Box 669, Mankato, Minnesota 56002.
www.capstonepress.com

Copyright © 2005 Capstone Press. All rights reserved.
No part of this publication may be reproduced in whole or in part, or stored in a retrieval system, or transmitted
in any form or by any means, electronic, mechanical, photocopying, recording, or otherwise, without written
permission of the publisher. For information regarding permission, write to Capstone Press, 151 Good Counsel Drive,
P.O. Box 669, Dept. R, Mankato, Minnesota 56002.
Printed in the United States of America

1 2 3 4 5 6 10 09 08 07 06 05

Library of Congress Cataloging-in-Publication Data
Dahl, Michael.
 Black: seeing black all around us / by Michael Dahl.
 p. cm.—(A+ Books. Colors)
 Includes index.
 ISBN 0-7368-3668-3 (hardcover)
 ISBN 0-7368-5070-8 (paperback)
 1. Black—Juvenile literature. 2. Color—Juvenile literature. I. Title. II. Series.
QC495.5.D34 2005
535.6—dc22   2004014354

Summary: Text and photographs describe common things that are black, including tires, hockey pucks, and black cats.

Credits
Blake A. Hoena, editor; Heather Kindseth, designer; Kelly Garvin, photo researcher

Photo Credits
Capstone Press/Gary Sundermeyer, cover, 3 (dirt, dominoes, sunglasses), 4–5, 6–7, 10–11, 12–13, 14–15, 20, 28, 29 (all),
    32 (dirt, eightball)
Capstone Press/Karon Dubke, cover, 3 (dog), 8–9, 16–17, 32 (dog)
Corbis/Matthias Kulka, 26–27
Gloria Muscarella/Cheval Photography, 24–25
Photodisc/G.K. Vikki Hart, 19, 22–23
Stockbyte, 18

Note to Parents, Teachers, and Librarians
The Colors books use full-color photographs and a nonfiction format to introduce children to the world
of color. *Black* is designed to be read aloud to a pre-reader or to be read independently by an early reader.
Photographs and activities help listeners and early readers understand the text and concepts discussed.
The book encourages further learning by including the following sections: Table of Contents, Glossary,
Read More, Internet Sites, and Index. Early readers may need assistance using these features.

Table of Contents

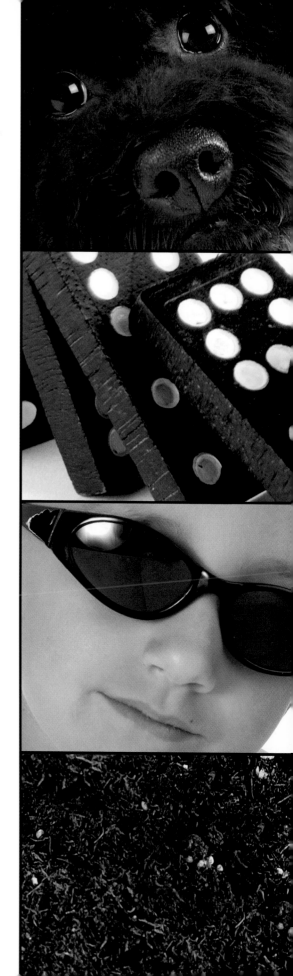

Black is where
a flower grows.

While hunting, the Inuit people used to wear whalebones as sunglasses. The bones had slits cut into them. They helped the Inuits see when bright sunlight reflected off ice and snow.

Black can sit upon your nose.

7

Black can sniff, snort, and sneeze.

A dog's sense of smell is about 1,000 times better than a person's sense of smell. Dogs can tell people apart just by sniffing them. Can you?

In the United States, nearly 300 million tires are thrown away each year. Making a tree swing is a good way to recycle an old tire.

Black swings beneath the trees.

Magician David Copperfield once performed a magic trick in which he made a jet airplane disappear.

Black is used for magic tricks.

Black tips over —
click, click, click!

14

In 2003, Ma Lihua of China broke a world record with dominoes. She set up and then toppled more than 300,000 dominoes.

Black slides
across the ice.

Professional hockey players can hit slap shots at nearly 100 miles per hour!

More Black

People in the United States believe that black cats are bad luck. But in England and Japan, people believe black cats bring good luck.

Black purrs and hunts for mice.

Billiard balls were one
of the first objects to
be made of plastic.

Black is shiny,
smooth, and round.

Beetles come in many sizes. A flea beetle is so small that it's hard to see. A darkling beetle (pictured) is about the size of a jelly bean. A Hercules beetle can grow larger than an adult's hand.

Black can crawl across the ground.

23

In 1877, the book *Black Beauty* by Anna Sewell was published. It tells the story of how a horse was treated by both mean and kind owners.

Black is beautiful, galloping by.

Black fills up
the starry sky.

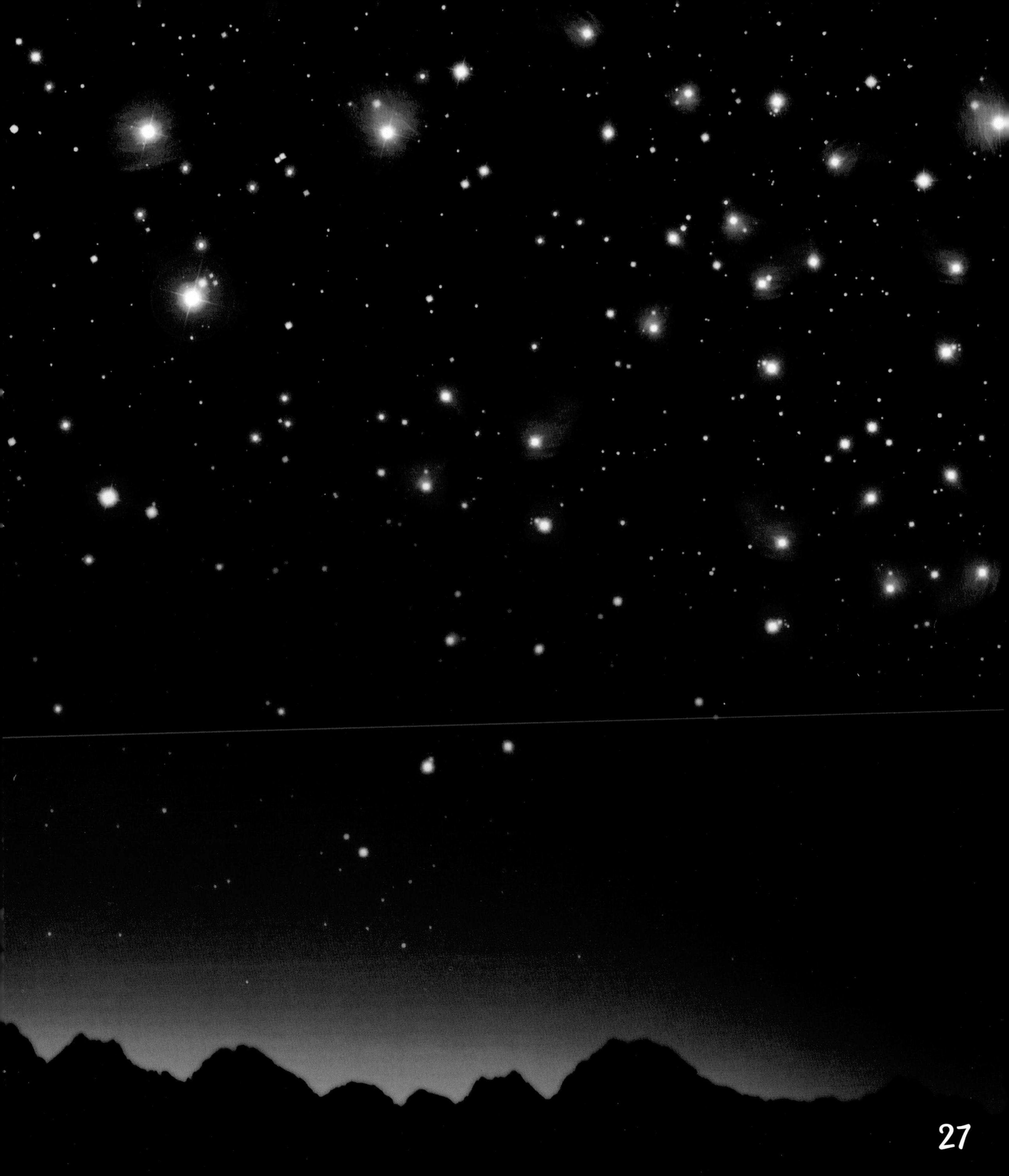

Making Shades of Colors

Artists use black to make colors darker. A darker hue of a color is called a shade.

You will need

paint tray

black paint

green paint

red paint

paintbrushes

paper

1 Put black paint in the middle of the paint tray. Add green and red around the black.

2 Using a paintbrush, move some of the red paint to a clean spot on the paint tray. Then add a very small amount of black to the new portion of red and mix the colors together. Notice how the red gets darker. Using a clean paintbrush, repeat this step with the green paint.

3 To make the shades of red and green darker, add very small amounts of black paint. When you're finished mixing, use the colors to paint your masterpiece.

Glossary

billiard (BIL-yurd)—having to do with billiards; billiards is a game in which people use a stick, called a cue, to hit balls around a table.

gallop (GAL-uhp)—to run fast; a horse gallops by lifting all four of its hooves off the ground as it runs.

hue (HYOO)—a color or variation of a color

plastic (PLASS-tik)—a strong, lightweight substance that can be made into different shapes, such as billiard balls, toys, and car parts

professional (pruh-FESH-uh-nuhl)—a person who makes money by doing something other people do for fun, such as playing ice hockey

publish (PUHB-lish)—to print a book

recycle (ree-SYE-kuhl)—to use old items, such as tires, aluminum cans, and newspapers, to make new items

reflect (ri-FLEKT)—to bounce off something

shade (SHAYD)—a darker hue of a color

topple (TAH-puhl)—to make something fall or tip over

Read More

Hidalgo, Maria. *Color.* Let's Investigate. Mankato, Minn.: Creative Education, 2003.

Mitchell, Melanie. *Black.* First Step Nonfiction. Minneapolis: Lerner, 2004.

Thomas, Isabel. *Black Foods.* The Colors We Eat. Chicago: Heinemann, 2004.

Internet Sites

FactHound offers a safe, fun way to find Internet sites related to this book. All of the sites on FactHound have been researched by our staff.

Here's how:
1. Visit *www.facthound.com*
2. Type in this special code **0736836683** for age-appropriate sites. Or enter a search word related to this book for a more general search.
3. Click on the **Fetch It** button.

FactHound will fetch the best sites for you!

Index